D0848074

FARM ANIMALS

Chickens

by Emily K. Green

BELLWETHER MEDIA • MINNEAPOLIS, MN

Note to Librarians, Teachers, and Parents:

Blastoff! Readers are carefully developed by literacy experts and combine standards-based content with developmentally appropriate text.

Level 1 provides the most support through repetition of high-frequency words, light text, predictable sentence patterns, and strong visual support.

Level 2 offers early readers a bit more challenge through varied simple sentences, increased text load, and less repetition of high-frequency words.

Level 3 advances early-fluent readers toward fluency through increased text and concept load, less reliance on visuals, longer sentences, and more literary language.

Whichever book is right for your reader, Blastoff! Readers are the perfect books to build confidence and encourage a love of reading that will last a lifetime!

This edition first published in 2007 by Bellwether Media.

No part of this publication may be reproduced in whole or in part without written permission of the publisher. For information regarding permission, write to Bellwether Media Inc., Attention: Permissions Department, Post Office Box 1C, Minnetonka, MN 55345-9998.

Library of Congress Cataloging-in-Publication Data
Green, Emily K., 1966–
  Chickens / by Emily K. Green.
      p. cm. — (Blastoff! readers. Farm Animals)
Summary: "A basic introduction to chickens and how they live on the farm. Simple text and full color photographs. Developed by literacy experts for students in kindergarten through third grade"—Provided by publisher.
  Includes bibliographical references and index.
  ISBN-13: 978-1-60014-064-8 (hardcover : alk. paper)
  ISBN-10: 1-60014-064-5 (hardcover : alk. paper)
  1. Chickens—Juvenile literature. I. Title.

  SF487.5.G74 2007
  636.5—dc22   2006035307

Contents

A chicken is
a kind of bird.
Chickens live
in groups
called **flocks**.

Chickens have feathers and wings. But they do not fly well.

A chicken has a
beak. A chicken
pecks for seeds
and insects on the
ground.

beak

A chicken has
a **comb** and
a **wattle** on
its head.

comb

wattle

11

A male chicken
is a **rooster**.
Roosters **crow**.

13

A female chicken is a **hen**. A hen lays eggs. A hen sits on the eggs to keep them warm.

15

Some eggs are
food for people.

Some eggs hold
baby **chicks**.

Baby chicks
grow up to be
chickens
on the farm.

Glossary

beak—the hard, pointed mouth of a bird

chick—a young chicken

comb—a piece of skin that grows on top of a chicken's head

crow—the call of a rooster

flocks—groups of animals that stay together

hen—an adult female chicken

peck—to pick at and eat small bits of food on the ground

rooster—an adult male chicken

wattle—a piece of loose skin that hangs from the throat of a chicken

To Learn More

AT THE LIBRARY

Scott, Janine. *The Rowdy Rooster*.
Minneapolis, Minn.: Picture Window Books,
2006.

Nelson, Robin. *From Egg to Chicken*.
Minneapolis, Minn.: Lerner Publications,
2003.

Zollman, Pam. *A Chick Grows Up*. New York:
Children's Press, 2005.

ON THE WEB

Learning more about farm
animals is as easy as 1, 2, 3.

1. Go to www.factsurfer.com

2. Enter "farm animals" into search box.

3. Click the "Surf" button and you will see a
   list of related web sites.

With factsurfer.com, finding more information
is just a click away.

Index

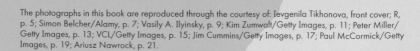